Perpetual Improvement

A Journey to Health, Wealth, Success, Happiness, and Great Relationships with the discipline of Fitness and good Nutrition

Michael Hartman

F,F,T

I would like to dedicate this book to my beautiful and loving wife who has supported me since the beginning of this Formal Fitness Training journey. I would also like to thank my parents who brought me into this world, provided me opportunities, and gave me everything they could. I would also like to thank my editor Matthew who truly helped me polish the writing. Lastly, I would like to thank all friends, family, and clients who have had any role in my personal growth, development, and success! This is just the beginning.

Thank you so very much!

Contents

Utilize what resonates with you and revisit the information often to keep improving and growing as an individual.

Enjoy the journey!

Introduction and Assessment: Current Life Assessment

"At Formal Fitness Training we believe in the relentless pursuit of health, wealth, success, happiness, and quality relationships achieved along with fitness and solid nutrition. It is our goal to improve the lives of our clients, friends, family, and people we have yet to meet through these principles."
– Michael Ray Hartman

"Shoot for the moon, if you miss you will land among the stars" – Les Brown

The only way to know where you currently are and where you want to go is through an assessment. I created one! If you don't assess, it's just a guess.

Before you read any further in this book, I would like you to take 10 minutes and take the "Current Life Assessment".

Across the top of your page write the following:

Health

Wealth

Success

Happiness

Relationships

Under each category I want you to give yourself a score of 1-10 indicating how well you are currently doing in that category. Be honest with yourself. A score of 1 being the worst that it could possibly be and 10 being the best that it could ever be in your wildest dreams. It is also important to point out that you should use your own value systems while doing this. If wealth to you is having a healthy family and plenty of food to eat you can consider yourself wealthy. If you think riches, money, and things are what causes wealth, give yourself a score based on that.

After you have your score out of fifty, double it which gives you your score out of 100%.

With your assessment completed, next take the subject which has the lowest number and spend the next month trying to bring it one point higher. As an example if success is a score of 3 where all the other numbers are 5; success would be the starting point.

To start improving, first write down reasons why you think you aren't as successful as you could be. Next write down things you can do to improve that area of your life in the next 30 days. You will continue doing this monthly until you achieve the numbers which you are striving for. If you'd like 9's in all categories is desirable then work towards 9's. If 7's is fine in your mind then that's your goal. If you want perfect 10's, buckle up and get it done! Each person who takes this assessment will use it in a different way, but the idea is to get you thinking about areas that can improve in your life.

Throughout this book we will cover how Formal Fitness Training defines health, wealth, success, happiness, and relationships. We will also discuss what it means to practice appropriate fitness and how solid nutrition serves as a backbone to achieve any and all goals in life.

In this book you will find many things designed to help you improve your life today. What you will not find is a guaranteed success formula. The tips in this book will still require you to make a change to improve.

Our system covered in this book (if utilized correctly) can improve your life exponentially. I challenge you to take the next calendar year to work towards an extraordinary life through improving your health, wealth, success, happiness, personal relationships, fitness and nutrition.

At the beginning of each month take the assessment again. Always focus on the areas with the lowest number first and work your way to improving all of your scores to at least 7's.

Example 1:

Health 5

Wealth 6

Success 5

Happiness 5

Relationships 5

= 26/50 (52%)

In this example you would start your 30 days of work on either health, success, happiness or relationships since wealth is at a 6.

Example 2:

Health 7

Wealth 7

Success 8

Happiness 3

Relationships 6

= 31/50 (62%)

In this example you would start your 30 days of work on happiness since it is the lowest score and you would spend the next three months trying to bring happiness up to relationships. Then you would choose between happiness or relationships to shoot for the next level which would be 7.

Example 3:

Health 9

Wealth 2

Success 3

Happiness 10

Relationships 7

= 31/50 (62%)

In this example you would start your 30 days of work on wealth since it is the lowest score then the following month you would choose between wealth and success. You continue working with the lowest scores until you get all five subjects up to a 7 or above.

Think about it, if you are at all 5's when you start and achieve a score of 50% and over the next twelve months you improve your assessment to all 7's you now have a passing score in this thing called life. From there keep growing and showing the world what you are made of.

If you are ready to go on this journey with me, and you have completed your assessment **turn the page**!

~ Thank you for choosing this book.

Michael Ray Hartman

Formal Fitness Training CEO

Chapter 1: The Story of Formal Fitness Training

"Do or do not, there is no try" – Master Yoda

I would like to tell you some of my story before I break down the five aspects of a successful life and how to utilize fitness and nutrition to get there.

Formal Fitness Training is the brainchild of many years of weight loss and struggles with injury. The Formal Fitness Training business launched because I saw things in the fitness industry that could be improved upon. The business may have never launched if not for a client at my first gym who believed in me. I had worked for a franchise gym for many years but coming off the 2011 recession this gym was forced to eliminate my position. They kept me on but with a major pay cut and no prospects for the future. It was at that time, that one of my clients wrote me a very generous check and handed it to me.

She said, "Mike you don't belong at this gym, you have so much more to offer. Take this money and start your own business".

This client helped me draw up the legal paperwork, assisted me with documents, and was there for me with any questions in the beginning and to this day. We no longer train together but I will always consider this person family because she believed in me deeply enough to give me a chance. To this day I don't know if I would have ever started my business if it wasn't for this remarkable human being.

Formal Fitness Training started by specializing in weight loss, muscle-building, and athletic performance. Our motto is "Strive for the best version of yourself." If you emulate someone else, you will fail, because there is only one you. Be your best by competing with yourself daily. The battle to win is the battle with the person you see in the mirror only! Formal Fitness Training has served over 500 clients with ten people who have lost over 100 pounds and twenty clients who have gained over forty pounds of muscle. We have seen clients from all walks of life and all occupations.

The Story

My name is Michael Hartman, and I am the owner and founder of Formal Fitness Training LLC. The beginning of this business came from years on the field and years in the gym! Throughout my life I played baseball from five to eighteen years of age and football from thirteen to seventeen. I always enjoyed hiking and street hockey as well. Staying active was never an issue for me, but I did struggle with proper nutrition. My parents involved me in as many sports as they could think of and they kept me active off the field also. Despite the involvement in activities and sports; however, I was still overweight, and being overweight as a kid is especially hard. I was tired of being called fat.

When I made it to high school I participated in yearly tennis and volleyball class, and a strength and conditioning classes. I was always lifting weights before or after school too. These activities allowed me to lose my middle school and early high school weight and put me at around 180 pounds. I looked good and felt as though I had some muscle. Unfortunately, that is where the story just begins.

Playing high school football, I was fielding an onside kick and took two helmets to the small of my back. This caused movement in my L3 and L4 (lower spine), developing a condition called Spondylosis. This injury caused a bend forward at the waist and forced me to stop football that season. Later I found out my football journey was over forever.

The doctor told me "This condition is manageable, if you put your mind to it and workout. The muscles will stay strong, and you will be able to manage this for the rest of your life. If you choose not to work out and keep the muscles fit, you may have serious problems as you age."

That was all I needed to hear. I went to physical therapy two or three times per week for around eighteen months to get myself standing tall and pain free again while my back returned almost to normal. After those eighteen months I planned to get myself back into the gym and back in shape and that is exactly what I did. The only trouble was I had gained considerable weight during physical therapy since the pain kept me from exercise. The injury left me at around 245 pounds.

So here I was between sixteen and seventeen years old (2003) with a back injury and around sixty more pounds of fat than I had prior to the injury. It was time to pay the sweat equity and get back in motion. I started doing two to three hours of exercise a day (this is not the way to do it) but over the course of about a year I was back to 180 pounds; however, I was very skinny and most of my muscle was gone. My diet was primarily chicken, salad, protein shakes and some fruit. It was time to start building some muscle again.

I spent my senior year of high school and freshman year of college putting on thirty pounds of muscle. It was a lot of fun having kids from high school tell me how much progress I had made. I followed a typical bodybuilding split with bodybuilding foods and supplements consisting of whey protein, creatine, amino acids, and caffeine. During this time, I also took a job at LA Fitness and enrolled in Penn State University for a B.S. in Kinesiology (2006).

I was looking good and feeling great, but then again slowly over time poor eating choices and the college grind led to about twenty excess pounds of weight gain. This wasn't due to an injury: it was simply due to a lack of self-control, and life. Remember, I always made sure to workout no less than five days per week from the day I talked to my doctor about my back injury. To this day I work out at least five days per week in the gym. After this second bought of weight gain, I decided I would lose the weight for good.

I spent seven years at LA Fitness before Formal Fitness Training was launched. All of my clients over the years have really inspired me to keep growing as an individual to keep working towards my own goals. My clients mean more to me than they will ever know from both a personal and professional perspective! Through my own struggles I have truly realized the compassion and love needed to help clients work through their struggles.

Arguably the best shape I ever achieved was when I lost about thirty-three pounds for my wedding which occurred on September 13th of 2014. This final weigh-in on the day of the wedding was 197 pounds. My joy is weight training so over 200 has become the normal for me because I enjoy lifting heavy weights and improving my performance which requires a steady dose of carbohydrates, fats, and proteins.

I now stand at about 215 pounds and I'm really focusing on keeping my diet clean these days. I do more cardio and continue to lift weights. I have found positivity in my life which really helps because the people in my life are very positive as well. I think that is a key to success.

The Chapter Yet to Come

My commitment to Formal Fitness Training and my clients is one that will never stop. I believe that I am on this planet to make people feel good, and to help people meet their goals.

There is a quote which I live by:

"I want to inspire people. I want someone to look at me and say, 'because of you I didn't give up.'"

If I have more people not quitting because of what I teach them, I will continue to be inspired to do better and to help more people.

Chapter 2: What is Optimal Health

"Success isn't always about 'Greatness.' It's about consistency. Consistent, hard work gains success. Greatness will come." – Dwayne Johnson

The thoughts that follow are life and experienced based. You will not find studies to support these nuggets of wisdom, but what you will find are tools that if utilized repeatedly will create lasting positive change in all aspects your life.

Optimal health is having appropriate blood pressure, cholesterol, function of your brain and organs; it is having minimal pain and discomfort while being free from disease or sickness.

More and more people are on prescription drugs today than ever before which is why it is so important to take control of your health from an early age, utilizing good nutrition and a dose of appropriate fitness to keep you healthy for as long as feasibly possible.

Health, however, goes much deeper than the aforementioned things. Health is the ability to sleep well, manage stress, stay hydrated, minimize alcohol consumption, avoid high smog areas, keep your air clean, keep your water clean, wash your food before consuming it, and buying the right foods. This is just a start for things you can do to keep your entire self moving in the right direction.

The best way to look at your body is like a car, and the best way to look at your mind is like a computer. If you give your body the right gas, oil, and additives, it will run smoothly and efficiently over time. If you feed your brain the right information and give it the correct commands, it will provide optimal performance and provide the answers you are looking for, for many years to come.

Throughout my fourteen years of personal training, I have found that optimal health amongst older people who have remained primarily healthy throughout their lives has come down to a few key things. So, here are the top five things I have found that contributes to longevity amongst my clients sixty years and older.

1. They consume fruits and vegetables daily and stay hydrated (80-130oz of water per day). They enjoy rich foods, desserts, and the occasional alcoholic drink but they don't overindulge.

2. They move and exercise consistently throughout the day and throughout the week.

3. They manage their stress and aim for 7-9 hours of sleep per night.

4. They see doctors yearly or regularly to keep tabs on what is going on with their body and health.

5. They spend time laughing and having fun daily and travel often.

When you look back to the assessment at the beginning of the book I said that what optimal health looks like to one person might look completely different to another but for the sake of this book I am going to give ten tips on things you can change today to improve your health RIGHT NOW and going forward.

1. Eat 5-7 servings of fruits and vegetables daily (organic if possible) and wash them before consumption. If you struggle to get that many servings in per day find a greens or reds superfood product to assist you and fill in the nutritional gaps. (www.1stphorm.com/fft) – I personally take Opti Greens 50 and Opti Reds 50 from 1st Phorm.

2. Get a high-quality water filter which removes 99% of the contaminants found in water. We personally use a filter which attaches right to a sink and provides three months of clean drinking water per filter.

3. Walk at least 30-60 minutes per day and spend more time standing. This will keep the body in the mode of activity instead of relaxation. Nothing will deplete your muscles or give you bad posture faster than sitting all day long. If you sit for work, get up and move around multiple times per hour even if it is just a few desk squats.

4. Find meals and food that you enjoy that are good for you. Create a weekly meal plan and then focus on trying to add some superfoods to your meals. Think cinnamon, nutritional yeast,

apple cider vinegar, flaxseed, nuts, ginger, garlic, oregano, etc....

5. Sleep 7-9 hours per night and find the amount that makes you feel refreshed when you wake up. If you wake up tired every day try adding 15 minutes to your sleep each week until you find your proper dose. I find 8.5 hours is perfect.

6. Weight train 2-3 days per week to strengthen the bones, muscles, ligaments, and tendons. Weight training has also been shown to help improve brain function.

7. Take a high-quality gender specific soft capsulated multi-vitamin and fish oil to fill in nutritional gaps in your diet. If you eat fatty fish 2-3 times per week you can omit the fish oil.

8. Try to avoid drama, which causes stress since stress causes health concerns.

9. Listen to music which you love. Find music that perks you up, mellows you out, inspires you, and makes you feel great. Then listen to it often! Generally, I listen to hard rock & heavy metal while working out, country music & reggae while at the beach, and acoustic music while I work.

10. Work on relaxation. Meditation, tiger tailing, stretching, foam rolling, massaging, mindfulness, reading, deep breathing, yoga, and reiki can all help you find a clean slate and

realize what true bliss and comfort in your own skin can feel like.

To grow in your health, you must grow in your daily routine. If your routine is designed to make you healthier, your routine is serving you, but if your routine is designed to make you sick, gain weight, or be inactive, your routine is hurting you.

It is best to hear what optimal health is from someone who has spent three quarters of a century living life. Enjoy this letter from a long-term client who works on optimal health daily.

"I have been blessed to have Mike Hartman as my trainer for three years. Our relationship has evolved to one of a deep, rewarding friendship. In the beginning, our conversations were very fitness-oriented, but over time, Mike now realizes the importance of considering the whole physical, emotional and financial well-being of his clients. I have benefited greatly from his guidance as I approach my 75th birthday!

I am a typical type-A personality and still working full time as a corporate travel consultant. I realize the satisfaction of working at a job that I enjoy as well as reaping the benefits of still receiving a salary and bonuses for a job well done. I enjoy many friendships among my clients, and that deepens my desire to ensure that their travel experience is worry-free. I have made a concerted effort to be debt free at this time in my life and concentrate on contributing to my 401-K and maintaining positive investment accounts.

I have been a widow for 10 years, and four years ago I made the decision to devote more time to self-care. My children are all active adults, and I was a rider in my younger years, so as I was aging, I realized the importance of staying flexible and working on my strength to maintain my bone density. I knew the best way to achieve these goals was to work with a personal trainer.

As I progressed, with professional guidance from Mike, I became stronger and improved my diet and endurance, all of which added to my overall wellbeing and contentment.

I can honestly say I enjoy working with Mike and truly enjoy the conversations we have outside of the realm of fitness. Mike really understands the benefits of working on the whole person, and that has added a wonderful dimension to my life. Taking into account the importance of exercise, diet, emotional and financial health is of value at any stage in life." – J.S.

This client has had such a positive impact on my life as well. She keeps me motivated and is always there for me as a source of mentorship, friendship, and even sometimes as a grounding source. I am so blessed to have high quality role models in my life through my clients. They keep me moving towards my goals, dreams, and aspirations. Life is meant to be enjoyed together, and I love continuing to learn and grow with those around me.

Chapter 3: What is Optimal Wealth

"You must gain control over your money or the lack of it will forever control you." -Dave Ramsey

What one person considers wealth and what another person considers wealth are two different things entirely. For the purpose of this book I will be looking at wealth strictly from a financial and money perspective. The other definitions of being wealthy (healthy family, happiness, and relationships) will be found in other areas of the book.

Growing up on the lower to middle end of middle class, I learned what it was like to not have a lot of extra money. We always had plenty of food to eat but throughout the years I had witnessed my parents struggle over money, and it seemed like there was never truly enough for my parents to live out their dreams. My dad woke up each morning and went to work. He rarely complained; he just filled his coffee mug and off he went. That is something that has stuck with me all these years: get up and go to work whether you want to or not.

My mom was more of the entrepreneur of the two. She was always looking to make money on side hustles which led her to eBay sales, Avon, Amazon, Etsy, and many other of those type of projects to make additional income for our family. My mom was truly best at working with elderly people, though, which taught me a lot about compassion, empathy, and emotional support. Throughout my early teens I would help her with meals on wheels and the local food bank. I would also assist her with activities at a local assisted living facility. Seeing her help the underprivileged and give all the people she encountered her whole heart was very inspiring. Delivering food and handing out bags to people in need so they could eat made me feel fulfilled.

Growing up with those morals but seeing that stress and anxiety around money made me realize a few things.

1. Money is so important because if you have enough of it you can help so many more people than if you don't have money.

2. You don't need money to make a difference: your time is important as well.

3. Bringing a group of people together to help others accomplishes a lot in a short period of time. A greater number of people working together to accomplish a specific goal (feeding people, building housing, etc.) provides energy and speed to get more done.

4. You will find no greater joy than the joy of giving someone a meal to eat when they otherwise wouldn't have one.

5. Stress around money can ruin lives and relationships so it is important to save, invest, and work hard to avoid those struggles.

As a personal trainer I am blessed to work with people of all walks of life. Each one of these people teaches me different lessons. I would like to share with you the five things I have learned from my most financially wealthy clients over the past fourteen years of personal training.

1. Save around 15% of your income and put it into a diversified portfolio to build wealth. This is also known as pay yourself first. (I stick with index funds and ETFs)

2. Be happy with what you have and don't spend frivolously. I find it important to point out that my wealthiest clients generally have the same two or three workout outfits and don't regularly come to the gym with new shoes and shirts for each workout.

3. Always have a cushion of 3-12 months of expenses accessible in an emergency fund to ensure when life happens you can stay out of debt and take care of the problem. (Washer dies, Microwave dies, TV dies, or you lose a job).

4. Stay out of debt. Some of them believe in leveraging debt to get ahead, but most of my clients over the years believe strongly in getting out of debt as soon as possible and then staying out of debt for the rest of your life.

5. Budget for the important things (kids' college, vacation, new homes, new appliances, etc.). If you know where your money is going you can plan for how to obtain your goals.

Those five things would be game changing, life altering advice to anyone who isn't currently doing those five things. Take some of those pieces and start working it into your life right now!

There is no secret as I write this book. I am only thirty-four years old which means the advice of my clients may be more grounded and backed by experience than the advice I'm giving, but what I have found so rewarding in my career is taking the clients younger than me, around the same age as me, and even sometimes clients older than me and personally inspiring them to do better with growing their wealth. Let's face it getting wealthy is fun, but getting wealthy along with your friends, family, colleagues, and clients is simply spectacular!

Along with training, I run a podcast called Coffee with a Trainer. The reason I do this podcast is because I believe in helping other trainers succeed. Collaboration over competition. We are supposed to be in this life together. Togetherness brings closeness, and closeness brings unity!

My tips for achieving financial wealth:

1. Save 5% of your income into a money market savings account always! (These accounts at the time of writing this are earning 2%. These won't make you rich, but they will help you build that emergency fund mentioned above.

2. Invest 15% of your income in a diversified portfolio of mutual funds. (I personally do an

   80/20 mix of stocks/bonds. In that portfolio I hold Real Estate REIT, Target Date Retirement Fund, Health Care ETF, Long Term Investment

Grade Bonds, Energy Fund, and Growth and Income Index.). Over the past six years people who are diversified could expect returns of 8-16%.

3. As you get older slow down on your stocks and opt for more steady and sustainable investments like bonds and fixed income indexes. (No need to do this until you are within 10-15 years of retirement).

4. Avoid the temptation of having the newest toys. New cars, new cell phones, new cutting-edge computers and TVs can destroy your opportunity to build wealth.

5. Sit down monthly and do a comprehensive budget with your significant other and make sure you know where all the money is going. This is where you see progress that was made over the past 30 days, and how you can budget money to achieve goals like vacation, sports camps, new apparel, etc.

6. Don't keep secrets from your spouse. Always be on the same page. Don't open separate credit cards that they don't know about, and always talk about purchases of $100 or more.

7. Go out to eat and enjoy life but make it part of your budget. I give myself $100 a week to spend however I like, but when it's gone, it's gone, and then I spend time in my most expensive asset......my house.

8. Drive a car that is a few years old. I've heard that the average millionaire drives a car that is about six years old. It is ok to buy new if you can buy it in cash and it doesn't affect your ability to invest or save the 20% per month.

9. Pay off your house early. That is my current goal. Paying a $200k mortgage off in fifteen years versus ten will save you around $100k.

10. Donate to charities, help people in need, and randomly give money to people you believe in. This is karma and good karma always comes back to you.

Those are some of the things that I have been using to help me grow my wealth and plan for my future, and I hope they help you do just the same!

Chapter 4: What is Optimal Success

"Successful people have a social responsibility to make the world a better place and not just take from it." – Carrie Underwood

So far, we have covered health and wealth and how it relates to the whole picture of improvement in life and growing as an individual. I think success might be the hardest topic within the assessment to evaluate honestly. To me success is based on how many people I've been able to positively influence: how many people have been inspired by me, learned from me, or taken information from me to improve their lives. Again, some could look at success as nice cars, giant yachts, huge homes, a freezer full of food, but for me success is the culmination of the honor, respect, love, and admiration that I have earned through helping others.

Throughout my personal training career, I have worked with over five hundred people and to my core I hope that they still utilize some of the things I taught them. To inspire others to be successful you must first inspire yourself to get motivated, stay motivated, and work on your own version of what optimal success is.

The clients I have worked with have achieved a multitude of successes in varying degrees and varying circumstances. I have trained millionaires, multi-millionaires, single parents, teachers, chief executives and financial officers. Of all these successful and influential people, I'm not sure who is best qualified to give tips on success, but of my clients who I believe to be at the top of their game, I've noticed they share these five attributes.

1. They give far more than they take. The provide value not only to their students, employees, and peers, but simply anyone they encounter. (Provide Value)

2. They truly care about others. When you see them meet someone, give a handshake, or give a hug, they really lean in and make the other person feel like they are the only person in the room. (Being Present)

3. They respect the opinions of others and give theirs in a non-judgmental way while highlighting points they believe to be important. (Respecting Other Opinions)

4. They share their knowledge providing shortcuts to success for others. (Sharing Knowledge)

5. They love. You know the people who when you meet them you can just tell that they love you as a human, as a person, and as a peer. They never look down on anyone who is less fortunate than them, and they are always empathetic, sympathetic, and there to help someone do better, feel better, or be better. (Loving Heart)

Those five attributes are a good starting point for how to be with all the people you interact with today. Once it becomes a habit it will become your normal, and your normal will then inspire other people to improve their normal, and from there the world improves.

To this point I have a set of values surrounding what I do with each one of my clients and how I try to be with them. In my life right now, this is what I look at as being successful.

1. Treat others with integrity and respect.

2. Give all your knowledge away to anyone who asks.

3. Be present and mindful of other's feelings.

4. Be a point of upliftment or support when someone is struggling.

5. Love others unconditionally knowing that no one is perfect and that you certainly are not either.

6. Give advice when asked, but always be providing nuggets of wisdom.

7. Lead by example be the change you want to see in the world.

8. Offer help—help people grab milk on the top shelf at the grocery store; help a friend move into an apartment, bring a meal to someone who just gave birth, so they don't have to worry about dinner. The possibilities are endless.

9. Be a networking source. You obviously don't know everything so it is important to always be building your network so people can find solid people through you to help them with things that you cannot.

10. Respect others. Don't judge; don't make assumptions, and always tell the truth. Respect for others is what gains respect for you.

Success is the constant pursuit and relentless effort to find consistent motivation, bountiful energy, and the knowledge required to seek a 1% improvement of your life and the lives of those around you each day!

"We often hear the cliché "Health is Wealth" All the money in the world doesn't matter if you're sick and can't enjoy life. Maintaining optimal health as we get older is vital to live a productive life.

As my husband and I approach our golden years we've come to realize how important regular exercising, proper nutrition, and restful sleep are in maintaining a productive lifestyle. Traveling, keeping up with the grand kids and engaging with friends, family and hobbies.

Mike helps keep us on track by working out two times a week. It's fun and increases the endorphins in the brain."

These clients inspire me very much because they started from humble backgrounds and worked their way a very successful life through hard work and determination.

The simple act of letting nothing stand in your way along with a solid work ethic, humility, an attitude of gratitude, and a progress mindset will together move you down the road of success!

Chapter 5: What is Optimal Happiness

"Carry out a random act of kindness, with no expectation of reward, safe in the knowledge that one day someone might do the same for you."- Princess Diana

Mindset

When I think of happiness, the very first thing that comes to mind is mindset. If you are in the wrong mindset every day you can find a reason to be unhappy, miserable, frustrated, negative, or think the world is out to get you. There are a few things which I have found really increase the odds of being unhappy. I offer my suggestions on how to minimize the damage caused.

1. The News – Watching the news increases your odds of being unhappy exponentially because most of the news is negative.

   Tip - I recommend avoiding the news or least try to stay informed while not letting news ruin your day.

2. Social Media – Social media has become the downspout of news. Through platforms like Instagram and Facebook, people fight about politics and religion; kids and adults make hurtful comments to each other.

   Tip - Social media can be used for good, but it can also be used for bad. I recommend limiting your time on each platform to about 15 minutes per day.

3. Being Negative – Try to always see the glass as half full versus half empty. Focusing on the positive on a regular basis can reframe your mindset for more growth.

   Tip - Try to stay positive as much as possible! People will start to wonder why you are happy all the time.

4. Being ungrateful – Don't take for granted all the great things you have in your life. Try to appreciate the simple things you have which many around the world do not have.

   Tip - Have an attitude of gratitude daily. Think of all the amazing things you have in your life. If you are reading this you probably have some extra money, a vehicle or two, a house, heat, air conditioning, clean drinking water, working plumbing, access to the internet, and a tooth brush which means you have a luxurious life compared to most people and countries in the world. Start acting like it!

Two things I would really like to expand upon are positivity and gratitude.

I have a challenge for you during the next thirty days regardless of what scores you achieved during your assessment. The challenge is to say thank you every morning and write down five things you are thankful or grateful for and say thank you before you go to bed and write down five great things that happened that day at school, work, or home. This will single handedly change your life. I have kept a gratitude journal for a year straight and sometimes I fall off the path of doing it, but I can assure you I see much more progress in my life when I say thank you and I write down ten things I am grateful for and good things that happened during that day.

As far as positivity, try to go the next seven days and when someone asks you how you are doing give them a quick grateful statement "I am truly doing well" or "I am blessed" or "I'm really good. Because let's face it: most days you will be doing well! You have made it through all the bad things that have happened in your life to this point and with the right attitude you will continue to push forward!

We can certainly have bad days, weeks, or potentially a bad month but I do not believe it is possible to have a bad year. Every time something bad happens learn from it and formulate a plan on how to not let it happen again.

Beyond Mindset

When you go beyond mindset, I look at happiness as contentment, motivation, mood, and Zen. The fluctuation of these four variables will determine how happy you are on that day. Happiness must come from within. I find happiness because I have spent the last eight years putting the past and mistakes behind me to keep moving forward and put systems in place to build my future.

Eight years ago, I was still acting and spending like I was in college, and I had amassed a DEBT fortune which I needed to work my way out of. I had college loans, a mortgage, credit card debt, a car loan, a furnace loan, an oil tank loan, a phone payment plan: I was seriously in a hole. I took the long way to get through that, and I just paid the minimums even when I had extra money, and I put off getting out of debt up until the beginning of 2018 when I decided enough was enough. I paid off about $47,000 in debt in about two years, because I got serious about it. I am now debt free except my home and I have some money put aside, and I think that being financially fit really makes a big difference in the opportunity to be happy. If my washing machine breaks, I buy a new one. Being financially stable turns a stressor into simply an inconvenience.

The reason I say this is because getting out of debt and growing up over those eight years required some major changes. Since I decided I was no longer going to live my life with debt, I needed to be happy with the things I had. I needed to be motivated to keep paying mass amounts of money to debt and keep positive while I was doing it. I needed to be at peace with where I was and where I was going. Anything in your life which makes you unhappy, if you look to those four things and alter your perspective you can start working towards happy.

Things to work on to be happy:

Contentment / Motivation / Mood / Zen

The funny part is the things that I put off buying or doing for two years to get out of debt are now things that I can work into my budget and buy whenever I want, because I'm no longer chained to interest payments.

> "Interest you earn is a gift, interest you pay is a punishment" – Chris Hogan

Throughout my fourteen years of personal training I have witnessed some extremely happy clients, and here are the five things that seem to be the golden rules for being happy I have learned from them!

1. Work – Do deeply meaningful work which you enjoy. This allows you to get up every day with a sense of purpose and passion to go get the job done. If you aren't currently doing something you love, work towards doing something you love. Start a side project with your full-time job, and then transition into a full-time career doing something which makes you happy!

2. Travel Often – The clients I know who are the happiest spend time at the beach, in the mountains and traveling the world doing the things they want to do. If we only get one life, we might as well enjoy it!

3. Faith – I've trained people from almost every religion but most of my happy clients have a religion, or something they believe in which is of a higher power or a greater energy than just themselves. Whether this is God, Source, Buddha, the Universe or something else, it seems to be very important.

4. Contentment – They are happy with what they have but always working towards what they want.

5. Rest and recovery – My clients who are the happiest take naps, get massages, take moments of pause throughout the day through meditation or just sitting still and thinking. They aim for appropriate amounts of sleep, and they are always looking for nutritional ways to boost their recovery and stay healthy.

Lastly in this chapter I will give the ten things that I do to stay happy.

1. Work: Do work which you absolutely love.

   - I do work which I absolutely love. I started Formal Fitness Training in 2011 and decided that I would no longer try to earn money on anything that I didn't enjoy. Today I have an apparel company; I promote 1st Phorm products; I do one on one training, group training, and online training; I coupon for my groceries; I invest; I save, and I still record music every now and again. Now as I am writing this, I am a writer as well and will soon be an author. I've been blogging for years. I absolutely love doing all those things which makes the work meaningful, impactful, and keeps me happy.

2. Love: Find the person who makes you happy and motivates you to do better and be more.

- I married the only person that I couldn't see myself living life without. My wife Meredith and I were friends two years before we ever dated, dated for around three years, got engaged, married, and have been together ever since. I had dated a few people over the years and even thought I was in love a few times, but I wasn't. During a moment of clarity when I had to decide, I tried to look to my future without Meredith, and all I saw was empty space. She enriches my life so much, and we truly enjoy each other (working out together, going to the beach, trying new breweries, going to new places, watching sports).

3. Hobbies: Find hobbies which fill your heart.

   - I am a guitar player, music enthusiast, and I like movies. I try to spend some time doing those things each week.

4. Purpose: Do things that make the world a better place and make you feel good.

5. Help Others: Go out of your way to give your knowledge to others so they can improve their lives.

6. Rest: Make sure you are well rested so you can perform at or close to your best all the time.

7. Travel: Make a list of places you want to go and make it happen.

8. Explore: Go out in the woods and take a hike; find some water and sit by it; go to new cities near you and walk around. Visit museums and monuments; attend plays; see a band. The possibilities are endless.

9. Exercise: Exercise daily even if it is for just 10-15 minutes and build up from there. Exercise is the best medicine and will keep you fit and able to do the things you love for many years to come.

10. Nutrition: Fuel your body with proper nutrition and your body will find happiness. If you have good energy and you try to find balance in the previous nine things, chances are you will be happy.

Most days you should be happy. If you are not, revisiting this chapter often to find ways to be happier. Progress over perfection is always the key, and happiness will always be a work in progress.

Chapter 6: What are Optimal Personal Relationships

"When people believe in you, you can do miraculous things"- Vin Diesel

The further we go in this book the more important each chapter becomes. In life I believe there is nothing more important than your personal relationships when it comes to development, happiness, contentment, and life satisfaction. When you live around toxic and negative people it creates a stressful environment putting your body in a constant state of chaos. When your body perceives stressors, it releases all sorts of fight or flight hormones such as cortisol and epinephrine which constricts the blood flow of the body and can cause things such as weight gain, high blood pressure, headaches, nausea, or even heart attacks or strokes. The stress hormones were originally intended for us to be able to run and hide from predators, not be upset about our family or friends who are judgmental and negative all the time.

I believe that you will become the financial and attitude average of the five or six people you spend the most time with. Take a moment to think about that for a few minutes. Who are your five or six? How much money do they make? Are they positive or negative? Do they fill you up or do they drain you when you are around them? Choose wisely!

A few years ago, I realized I needed to take a close look at my relationships. I had my family, a great relationship with my wife, and great relationships with my clients but I realized that I let my friendships slip due to building my business and prioritizing that. Since then I have made it a point to work out with a friend or two each week, go out for coffee with someone at least once per month, and I make it a point to spend at least one Saturday out and about with friends in each thirty day stretch. This has really led to solidifying some relationships that had slipped because of my schedule.

When someone asks you for a few moments of your time, try to accommodate them. Sometimes all they need is a few minutes not a whole day. A simple 'hello' through text message or a five-minute conversation on the phone or in person can completely change the trajectory of someone's day.

In this chapter I'm going to first give you what I think quality personal relationships should look like, and then I will analyze my successful clients in the realm of personal relationships and share what I see that they do to cultivate these great bonds.

The ten things that make a great personal relationship:

1. Time – If you want to have great personal relationships, the most important thing is time. I'm not just talking about time spent, but the quality of time spent. Thinking back on my best friends, we have always made time for each other. Make time for those you love!

2. Respect – All of your friends are going to go through some stuff from time to time that will alter their mood, behavior, or attitude. It is your responsibility to be there for them during these times. It can be a death in their family, the

death of a pet, a breakup, loss of job or any number of things but true friends will always respect the struggle and success of their friends and be there for them. You should be there to lift your friends up when they are down and keep them going strong when they are doing well. Another component of respect is being truthful and trustworthy. If someone loves, you enough to tell you a secret, it is your responsibility to keep it. Be respectful!

3. Inspiration – I believe you should be an inspiration to your friends. If a friend tells you a new idea or business venture, it is your job as a true friend to ask questions and support whatever they are trying to do. Be an inspiration!

4. Compassion – Being compassionate during times of need will forge bonds that are unbreakable. My closest friends have supported me through so many ups and downs. Always try to put yourself in someone's shoes when they are telling you something important. Be compassionate!

5. Loyalty – Loyalty takes a lot of shapes. When someone makes a mistake, it is all too easy to throw them away like yesterday's left-over chicken, but those are the times when you must show loyalty. Everyone is going to have weak moments. During weak moments when someone's personality is altering, you should focus on the bonds you have with them: that will support your ability to stick by your friend during their tough times. Be loyal!

6. Love – I think this is the most important component of a healthy relationship. Always lead with love. Love your fellow humans; love animals; love the environment: these are the quickest ways to turn this world into a better place. Treat others like you would treat your best friend whether you like the person or not. Look someone in the eye and make a bond even if it's only a few moments. Being the one to hold a door for someone or tell them they are doing a great job can be the difference between that person going home happy or going home sad. Love your friends, your neighbors, and strangers. Love always!

7. Motivation – The ability to motivate someone is huge, because today distractions are everywhere. The strain on our time comes from devices, workloads, and even long commutes. Staying motivated can be hard. Being the reason, someone is motivated today will make you feel great! If a friend is struggling, find the root of the problem, and help motivate them or give them some ideas on how to move forward with the dilemma. Be a motivator!

8. Good listening skills – With cell phones, tablets, and computers constantly vying for our attention, I find it more important than ever to talk to each other. Nothing is sadder than going out to dinner and seeing a family of four or a group of friends texting other people when they are in public with each other. As a business owner it is easy for me to fall into this trap as well. Still, I try my hardest to avoid staring at my phone when I'm with others. Quite simply,

it's disrespectful to ignore somebody else for a phone. If you are waiting for a call or text, make sure to alert your friends or family that you may need to take a call. That at least gives them a head up! Good listening skills require effort. Leaning into a conversation and letting the other person speak and finish before you speak is the most important. Also meeting the person at a similar volume is important. Talking loudly to someone who is a quiet speaker really throws the equilibrium of that conversation off tilt. Listen, understand, then respond!

9. Commitment – As I said above sometimes time isn't everything in a relationship: sometimes it's just commitment. Commitment is the ability to see things through, when life is going well and when life is going badly. Commitment is moving things around in your schedule to be there for someone's football game, graduation, wedding, funeral, etc.... It's never easy, but if you strive for a quality network of people in your life, commitment is very important.

10. Sacrifice – Sacrifice much like commitment is giving up something you want to do for something that you should or need to do. Think about this. No one enjoys moving, and no one enjoys helping someone move. However, there are few things that show someone you care more than sacrificing some time to help them do something which they know is not exciting for you to be doing.

These pointers are just a starting point, but if you think of your relationships and then write down the last time you did any of those ten things for the most important people in your life, you will identify areas that are a strength, and also areas that can be improved upon.

Next I would like to share what my friends, family, & clients do for me that I identify as the five most important things that show me, they care. In fourteen years of training I have found myself extremely blessed to share bonds with clients who always keep me motivated and moving forward. I am a lot to handle with ideas coming from all over all the time, but my clients know this about me and many of them try to help me stay focused.

1. Knowledge – My clients have always been willing to show or teach me what they know which proves that they do this in other relationships in their lives as well. I find it very important to ask questions and learn from those around you as a way of moving forward and continuing to grow as an individual.

2. Motivation – As a business owner motivation can be an up and down endeavor but my community has always helped me to stay motivated. I have a client who must use a walker, and he has a care aid who helps him get around. Nothing motivates me more than seeing him continue to try despite his injuries. Being a motivation for others is key to building quality relationships and will really inspire others to do more. Motivation is key.

3. Listening – We all know someone who doesn't listen: they speak over you and always need to be the

center of attention. That is not the way to be if you want to have great relationships. People who are the best listeners are also the ones who give the best advice and can move pieces of the puzzle around to make things fit better for others.

4. Genuine – People who are authentic or genuine are those who will be important people for your life: they are the people who are always unapologetically themselves. We all know that sometimes we alter our personalities to cater to differing personalities, but that is not something that should be done on a regular basis. It is better to gravitate towards the ones who show you their truth.

5. Nurture – What is nurture versus nature? There are hundreds of books devoted to trying to prove whether genetics are a component of nurture (you eat the same things and have similar beliefs) or nature (inherited or cellular). It has been said in many ways that you will become the average of a certain number of people you surround yourself with both financially, mentally and physically. It is important to nurture people to improve or do better when they try new things or are pursuing something beyond their normal. Being nurturing is to help with ideas, supporting decisions, and offering advice if asked.

Relationships will always have ebbs and flows, ups and downs, excitement and disappointment, but it is my hope that this chapter gives you some ideas on how to become a better friend, family member, or person to everyone which you encounter. Keep moving towards improvement always with an onward and upward mindset.

Chapter 7: What does Fitness have to Do with Life Improvement

"You miss 100% of the shots you don't take" – Wayne Gretzky

Throughout this book we have covered health, wealth, success, happiness, and personal relationships and how I personally have improved those areas of my life and how high achieving people in my life have shown me to keep improving. As a personal trainer and owner of Formal Fitness Training I need to give some tangible advice on how to improve your fitness and nutrition so that you can be fit, energetic, pain free and sharp minded.

I do not currently know any ultra-successful people who do not have a component of fitness in their lives. Most successful high achieving people who you would "Google" would return links to their exercise programs or routines that allow them to be successful. Try Googling "Jennifer Aniston workout routine" or "Dwayne Johnson diet".

Fitness has saved my life single handedly more than anything else. Injuries were a giant component of my ups and downs. As a baseball and football player for years I experienced a multitude of setbacks. During an onside kick I suffered an L3 and L4 lower back injury from a massive collision; I broke my fibula colliding with a catcher; I've twisted my ankles more times than I can count; I've had broken fingers, a partial rotator cuff tear, a partial ac joint tear, a pectoralis minor strain, bone spurs in my knee,

knee and hip discomfort, elbow strain and more. Only a few of those occurred while lifting weights while most of them occurred playing sports. If you are a current athlete or if you were in athletics previously, I am sure you can relate!

The thing that remained steadfast was that after each injury I was back in the gym "Clanging and banging" (Dwayne Johnson) the weights and getting my body back to its original form. With every set back comes the opportunity for new muscle and more improvement of the body. Clients who hurt themselves at work always inspire me to keep them motivated because I know that an injury is just a setback with a massive opportunity to fine tune your body to be stronger because of it. Injuries come from weak links in the body which is why it is important to leave no stone unturned. (Every muscle, ligament, tendon, bone, and tissue are important).

Here are the top ten pieces of fitness advice I can give you to improve your fitness now. These are pretty simple, and I won't go into great detail on them, but if you are looking to expand upon this you can find me at www.formalfitnesstraining.com or at varying gyms around Berks county. I also do online training.

1. Do not sit for more than thirty minutes without getting up and at least walking around the room.

2. Stretch daily even if it's just for a few minutes.

3. Weight train two to three days per week. If you currently are not weight training start with one day and build up to three.

4. Perform thirty to sixty minutes of walking throughout each day. It does not have to be all at once.

5. Get a monthly massage to keep your body operating at its best.

6. Perform movements at home or in the gym that work all muscles of your body. Choosing eight to ten exercises per workout should do the trick.

7. Learn how to do abdominal planks and bird dogs and do them for five minutes total multiple times per week. A strong abdomen and lower back will have you moving better throughout your day.

8. Utilize good form when picking anything up. Picking up a pen improperly can throw your back out.

9. Learn how to foam roll and roll your body multiple times per week for 5-10 minutes.

10. Park your car as far away as possible from the store and walk to the store. Leave the front spots for people who have legit injuries. Break the inertia of laziness and do this from now on. It amazes me when I see people driving around the parking lot looking for the closest space.

In the last part of this chapter I will tell you the five things I have found my clients share as their biggest accomplishments from personal training and improving their fitness.

1. They experience less overall back pain and better overall movement.

2. They achieve better sleep throughout the night.

3. They possess more energy throughout the day.

4. Their mind functions better with more clarity and focus.

5. They experience less injuries and setbacks with the ability to better perform their passions and their jobs.

Just imagine if you experienced less back pain, moved better, had great sleep, possessed bountiful energy, and had a sharp mind. Wouldn't giving these fitness tips a try, be worth it to gain those benefits? What are you waiting for?

*Disclaimer: If you have not been currently exercising it is a good idea to go visit your doctor and make sure you are ready for increased physical activity.

A message from one of our Clients:

"Put your health first. I found out that exercise gives me energy to get through my day. I am more alert and able to achieve my goals each day. Regular exercise helped me to be disciplined at work and be successful and happy in my life" – B.L

Chapter 8: What does Nutrition have to do with Life Improvement

"Our food should be our medicine, and our medicine should be our food" – Hippocrates

Health is wealth and solid fundamental nutrition is the greatest way to achieve good health. The foods that are healthy for us are the same foods which were healthy hundreds of years ago but for some reason we keep reaching for highly processed food. The fat burner and supplement industry keeps growing into a larger industry with each passing year. What is the reason for that? People are looking for a quick fix with regards to improving their nutrition and diet. Don't get me wrong: supplements have their place to fill in nutritional gaps, but fat burners in my mind have zero place in the cabinets of consumers.

Throughout this book we have gone over countless ways to improve your life but some of these things require time. If you don't have good nutrition, you won't have good health, and that may mean your time on this planet could be limited. Did that scare you? I hope so.

Your diet should evolve with your goals and with the needs of your aging body. The calories and nutrients you needed as a sixteen-year-old are not the same calories or nutrients you require as a sixty-year-old. If you know your diet needs a giant overhaul, I recommend meeting with an experienced registered dietician or at least a fitness professional who can give you tips on improvement.

If you have any special nutritional needs or dietary restrictions it is very important that you see an allergist and nutritionist to make sure your individual needs are being met.

Here are the ten things that I have found to be the fundamentals for nutrition. I train many people over the age of sixty who can run laps around people I know in their twenties and thirties. If you get something out of this chapter you will be well on your way to living a robust life and increasing your longevity.

1. Eat five to seven servings of different colored fruits and vegetables daily, the more colors, the more diversified the nutrition. Much like the stock market, index fund your fruits and vegetables with different intake each week! Try a new fruit today, try a new vegetable tomorrow.

2. Limit intake of sugar, alcohol, salt, and dairy. (Opinions vary but I believe this should all be consumed in moderation while having some additional fun occasionally.)

3. Drink at least half your body weight in water per day. A 200-pound person should consume 100oz of water daily. Also include 16oz for each additional hour of physical activity each day. Coffee, protein shakes, juice, and other beverages also count towards this goal. (alcohol does not)

4. Choose organic fruits, vegetables and grass-fed beef. Eat heritage raised pork, wild caught

fish, and free-range chicken and eggs if you can afford it. Farmers markets usually have great less expensive options. I also like Butcher box!

5. Eat mixed nuts if you are not allergic, along with avocados and extra virgin olive oil for the bulk of your fat intake. Nuts are rich in heart healthy mono and polyunsaturated fats.

6. Ignore the low carbohydrate advice. If you are active you need carbohydrates for your mind and performance. Aim to have most of your carbohydrates before or after your workouts and reduce intake closer to bedtime. Matching your carbohydrates to your activity level is important. Someone who sits most of the day requires far less carbohydrates than a marathon runner.

7. While it doesn't involve nutrition directly, be sure to sleep seven to nine hours per night. Naps of twenty to thirty minutes are also good.

8. Take a gender specific soft capsuled multi-vitamin to fill in any nutritional gaps you may be missing out on in your diet. The needs of men and women are different, so gender specificity is key.

9. Get blood work done to check your iron, Vitamin-D, testosterone, blood sugar, cholesterol, blood pressure and more so you can tweak your diet to make it optimal. Based on your gender and age your doctor will know

which tests are the most important to keep a close eye on.

10. Have fun with nutrition. Try new meals; learn how to cook different things; eat something new each week, and experiment. If you keep nutrition fresh it won't be nearly as boring, and you will stay motivated to keep progressing in the improvement of your health! Check out Pinterest for new recipes.

What I have found to be the most impactful with nutrition is variation. The more you try and the more you learn, the better and more exciting your nutrition and your meals will be. Many of my clients go to different stores and farmers markets to get different foods to keep their nutrition fresh and not boring. Almost all the clients I train over the age of sixty follow these ten tips and then they fill in their nutritional gaps with high quality supplements.

Final Thoughts

"Peace begins with a smile" – Mother Theresa

      This book is by no means a be-all and end-all source for ways to improve your life. Much of your personal growth and discovery in all avenues of health, wealth, success, happiness, and relationships will be a mission of self-discovery. It is my hope that these tools will at least make you think, make you try to be better, make you try to do more, and have you inspiring others. Go out each day and try to make others better; help others do more, and help others open their mind to giving and improving. Fitness and nutrition are the vital key because without health, you cannot help others, and without fitness you will not move well so your impact will be diminished.

      In 2011, Formal Fitness Training began as a fitness company designed to help people get in shape, and it has now morphed into something much bigger. I cannot begin to express the gratitude I have for all the support that the community has shown me. On our own we can improve, but together we can make the world a better place. Onward and upward always!

About the Author

Michael Hartman is a professional trainer who has fourteen years of experience training people of all ages. Michael started Formal Fitness Training on August 15th of 2011. Michael holds a B.S. in Kinesiology from Penn State University, and his NSCA-CPT certification. Michael strives to create a positive environment for all his clients to grow and succeed in all areas of health, wealth, success, happiness, and personal relationships. All this growth is obtained through solid components of personal development, fitness and good nutrition.

Website: www.formalfitnesstraining.com

Email: Michael.hartman6@gmail.com

Facebook: www.facebook.com/formalfitnesstraining

Supplements: www.1stphorm.com/fft

Podcast: https://anchor.fm/coffeewithatrainer

Information and Knowledge Resources

www.breakingmuscle.com

www.sciencedaily.com

https://www.edmylett.com

https://www.andyfrisella.com

https://www.mindbodygreen.com

https://www.ncbi.nlm.nih.gov/pubmed/

Recommended Podcasts

The Dave Ramsey Show

Chris Hogan's Everyday Millionaires

The Ed Mylett Show

The Joe Rogan Experience

Gary Vaynerchuk

Dave Meltzer's – The Playbook

The EntreLeadership Podcast

Recommended Reading

Money and the Law of Attraction – Jerry and Esther Hicks

The Total Money Make Over – Dave Ramsey

Everyday Millionaire – Chris Hogan

Tribe of Mentors – Tim Ferriss

Tools of Titans – Tim Ferriss

Principles – Ray Dalio

Unshakeable – Tony Robbins

The Encyclopedia of Modern Bodybuilding – Arnold Schwarzenegger

Relentless – Tim S. Grover

The Universe Has Your Back – Gabrielle Bernstein

Stop Doing That Sh*t – Gary John Bishop

The Magic – Rhonda Byrne

Lifespan – David Sinclair

The Four Agreements – Don Miguel Ruiz

Made in the USA
Monee, IL
26 February 2020

22188261R00035